THE 12 ASCENSION PRINCIPLES

THE COVENANT BETWEEN SCIENCE AND SPIRITUALITY

K.C. Bass

© Copyright 2020 – K.C. Bass

All rights reserved. This book is protected by the copyright laws of the United States of America. This book may not be copied or reprinted for commercial gain or profit.

Scriptures marked KJV are taken from the KING JAMES VERSION (KJV): KING JAMES VERSION, public domain.

Scripture quotations marked MSG are taken from *THE MESSAGE*, copyright © 1993, 2002, 2018 by Eugene H. Peterson. Used by permission of NavPress. All rights reserved. Represented by Tyndale House Publishers, a Division of Tyndale House Ministries.

TABLE OF CONTENTS

Chapter 1 1
Principle One: Spiritual Consciousness

Chapter 2 8
Principle Two: Your Humanity

Chapter 3 13
Principle Three: The Science of God

Chapter 4 18
Principle Four: Science and Spirituality

Chapter 5 23
Principle Five: Alignment

Chapter 6 28
Principle Six: Assignment

Chapter 7 33
Principle Seven: Allowing

Chapter 8 38
Principle Eight: Authenticity

Chapter 9 42
Principle Nine: Law of Attraction and Lawof Faith

Chapter 10..47
Principle Ten: Evolution

Chapter 11..53
Principle Eleven: Cultured for Ascension

Chapter 12..60
Principle Twelve: Miracles, Signs, and Wonders

CHAPTER 1

PART I - 12 PRINCIPLES OF ASCENSION

PRINCIPLE ONE: SPIRITUAL CONSCIOUSNESS

What does it mean to become spiritually conscious or spiritually aware? Some define this in the context of their relationship with God. Others use their relationship with their religion or their relationship with whatever they deem to be the supernatural authority in their life. Allow me to share my story of how I became spiritually conscious—I promise I will give you the short version (LOL).

I was born into an 18-year-old mother. By no means was my birth a mistake; I believe God gave me both my parents to help usher me into the world. My mother married in her early twenties. We had always gone to church, my grandmother and I were always learning about God. As I grew into a teenager and began to learn more about the baptism of the Holy Spirit taught in the Christian faith, I entered prayer to experience this supernatural power. I received the baptism of the Holy Spirit at 18; the same age as my mom when she had me. I then awakened to the awesomeness of the power of the comforter.

From that day to this one I have been guided by the Holy Spirit. I have seen supernatural manifestations in the form of miracles, healings, and divine favor. No one can make me doubt the power of the Holy Spirit, mainly because I have had my own encounters. I coupled the encounters with the study of the word of God, which indeed has strengthened my discipleship journey. I have not been the only one that has recognized this supernatural awakening from within.

Many scientists have also revealed research on the validity of spiritual consciousness. Most will share that there is an intelligence working behind the scenes, which causes everything to exist. They may not call it the Holy Spirit, they may call it a source of divine intelligence, but I know exactly what they mean.

I listened to a TedTalk by Clinical Scientist Dr. Lisa Miller. She spoke about 15 minutes or more about her spiritual awakening and how her longing to birth a child led to her depression from grief. After many in vitro attempts, no baby. It led her on a spiritual journey to connect with those like her that were in grief but could connect with a spiritual presence that seemed to keep showing up at the darkest of times. She described the depression as two sides of a door.

Now, she wasn't speaking about clinical depression. She was speaking of transitional depression. Though she didn't name it, that was the best name I could come up with to describe it.

One side of the door was the despair of not having the love of a child to a parent. It was a deep, dark, carved out pit with no light. On the other side of the door, there was a bright light of possibility and solution. See, during this time of her spiritual journey, she spoke of what she called a presence asking her a question, "If you were pregnant, would you adopt?" As she delved deeper in her spiritual journey and she was able to say yes to that question, not only did the doors open for her to adopt, but she also conceived a daughter.

She realized that in her search for what she longed for, she found something greater that opened her heart up to a love that couldn't be explained. It was a flawless stream of unconditional love. The same love she felt with what she called presence was the same love she had for both her children. The years of barrenness forced her into a portal of spiritual consciousness. This is the very portal that we all have to experience in order to become spiritually aware.

I do a great job in not debating what people name God. I accept that they have the choice in what spiritual path they choose. I also honor the fact that people are awakening all over the world.

From a scientific standpoint, we are vibrational beings. We resonate constantly and we never stop. It is that part of us that connects with the Holy Spirit or as Dr. Miller stated, with presence. It is this open, allowing, receptive mode that lets us live fully and certainly love fully. It helps you to engage with the Creator within. It is our tapping into what I would call the spirit realm and others would call aligning their energy centers. I can not discredit their path or journey because I only know mine. I am only a master of the journey I have chosen. Everyone is going through their own stages of spiritual development.

Let's view it from another perspective. An acorn develops into a tree and we don't water it or make it grow. It grows on its own. The lilies in the field grow and blossom in the wind but not because we planted them. Our hearts beat, eyes blink, blood flows through our body, and its not because we are controlling those functions. You would have to know that there is a creative intelligence, I call it the Holy Spirit. The creator of all things is God. We can't dispute that we have too much evidence to support it. It is by no human means that we can breathe, walk, talk and grow from an infant to an adult. It is when we tap into that flow that we become one and enter the relationship with what is divine.

We use tools to enter that sacred place, such as prayer, meditation, stillness, and nature. You pick a tool and then use it to go into that sacred place. I recall attending an India Arie concert with a friend of mine. Her song "Sacred Space" resonated with me so much. As a deeply spiritual person, what resonated at her concert was an element of love and peace. It was a calmness that permeated through the place; it was indeed a sacred space.

Let's move further into an area where more Western Christians can relate. Ever heard of the lost books of the Bible?

I am sure you have. These are the Gnostic books. By definition the word means "relating to knowledge" and/or especially esoteric mystical knowledge. There was a reason these books weren't canonized to be included in our King James Version Bibles. It introduced a more mystical side of Jesus. Now, don't go left, stay with me. The Gospel of Thomas V3 states (The Gnostic Gospels of Jesus, Marvin, Meyer, Republished by Gnostic Society Library)

(3) Jesus says:

- (1) "If those who lead you say to you: 'Look, the kingdom is in the sky!' then the birds of the sky will precede you.
- (2) If they say to you: 'It is in the sea,' then the fishes will precede you.
- (3) Rather, the kingdom is inside of you and outside of you."
- (4) "When you come to know yourselves, then you will be known, and you will realize that you are the children of the living Father.
- (5) But if you do not come to know yourselves, then you exist in poverty, and you are poverty."

Here Jesus says according to Thomas that the Kingdom is INSIDE OF YOU and OUTSIDE OF YOU! So, when we deal with consciousness, we can't leave out the inner focus. The disciples were looking for directions on where the Kingdom was. He continues to say that when you COME TO KNOW YOURSELVES, THEN YOU WILL BE KNOWN…Literally you have to embrace the inner part of you to come to the realization of what is being manifested outwardly.

This is hidden only to those who don't seek. Coming to know yourself is coming to know who you are spiritually. Knowing the power you possess and embracing that the Kingdom is realized within and without.

So what is your story? When did you awaken to that greater One on the inside? Was it at a church or at a meditation retreat? Was it in your home when you received divine instruction or riding in your car? We all have a story of the sacred space of our lives. The key is to allow that space to cause you to ascend to higher dimensions of love and flow. You can not ascend to those dimensions without being spiritually conscious.

As an individual that embraces my prophetic grace, it is impossible for me to hear the Holy Spirit if I am not in touch with my Creator. I entered a relationship those many years ago as a child. I remember sitting in my closet with the door closed, just talking to God. I would feel so much love that surrounded our conversations. Every human being desires to be bathed in that unconditional love. It is the driving force for our connectivity. The more spiritually conscious you are, the more deeply guided and led you become. You are more authentic and bold in just being you. It is what we should all be attaining daily.

Ascension happens automatically for the spiritually conscious individual. The sky isn't the limit because there are no boundaries in the rise. ☺

PROPHETIC DECREE: YOU HAVE LEAPED INTO SPIRITUAL CONSCIOUSNESS AND YOU HAVE EMBRACED HEARING PROPHETICALLY.

CHAPTER 2

PRINCIPLE TWO: YOUR HUMANITY

What exactly does it mean to be human? Well, if we go over with anatomy, we can safely say we have two legs, two arms, two eyes, and two ears. We have ten fingers and toes, one heart, one liver, two lungs, two kidneys, and one gall bladder. We have a nervous system, circulatory system, endocrine system, digestive system, muscular system, and reproductive system. We also have an immune system, excretory system, skeletal system, respiratory system, cardiovascular system, and integumentary system. We carry around other organs but you get my point (LOL).

I would say that being human is a wonderful thing. We are the most advanced of all mammals and are able to perform tasks that set us apart from the average German shepherd or rhino. We are equipped with the capability to apply emotions to our everyday comings and goings. We can intelligently build nations and worlds. We are technologically advanced, and basically we are the bomb.com (LOL).

So you may be asking what does this have to do with ascension? It is actually a catalyst of ascension. Ascension requires that you be in tune with your humanity. Your fears, joys, pain, and lessons. All of this is your emotional humanity. Physically, if are in pretty good health then your physical body doesn't pose a problem. However, let's explore being emotionally bankrupt.

I can recall many times in life when I felt emotionally bankrupt and loathing my humanity. I battled depression for about ten years until I stepped into total healing. My encounters with the Holy Spirit and my therapist worked a sure miracle. I never had to take medication and from that healing to this day I have been free. During the times I was suicidal and depressed, I was emotionally drained. I was fully living in my humanness. My emotions were my guide and they didn't guide me well. I was living as a single parent of two rambunctious boys and had gone through a devastating divorce. It was not in the plan, people. No one gets married to get divorced.

So, at 25 I was staring it right in the face. What was I going to do? How was I going to survive financially? How was I going to make it out of this ok? I nursed those thoughts daily and into the hole of depression I went. It was a dark, lonely place. I can recall times my five-year-old would lay his little hands on my head and pray for me. I had taught him at a very young age how to pray and he was and still is a gifted young man. My woes of single parenting, my financial deficits, my emotional instability had me living in my humanity without a blueprint to get out.

I felt trapped in a life that was a dead end. I had to rely on the Holy Spirit to lead me and guide me during those years. I reached out to a therapist at that time and it was at that moment that my life took a turn for the better. I am a fierce advocate of mental health. I saw the change in my thinking with talk therapy. I had to revisit hard places in my life. I had to relive grueling events in my life, but I was able to walk out of my depression without pills, without long-term treatments. I was healed of depression and I have never returned to it. I had to couple my humanity with my spirituality. I had within me the key to healing but wasn't tapping into it. I didn't go to a Christian therapist, I went to a person I didn't know, who wasn't going to spiritualize my issue. In the end I was directed right back to the source of healing without her making one reference to the Holy Spirit. I no longer felt trapped. I felt expanded and free. She encouraged me to journal and I found it to be the tool that led me to realizing that there was a writer in me.

Another experience I had with my humanity is tunneling through rejection and the emotions that were attached to it. We all have experienced some sort of rejection in this life. I believe out of every 5 people, 4 have experienced it; it's just my analysis. It is very common. At that period in my life, it was easy for me to believe low-frequency thoughts of myself because I wasn't accepted in different arenas. Whether it be by absentee parents, cliques, on our jobs, or in relationships, rejection can affect the way we see ourselves. Each time rejection would come, it was like it added another layer to my dysfunctional thinking. Rejection will make you defensive. You will feel you have to defend every single part of yourself. Your ideas, your decisions, and your moves seem to be under constant scrutiny. The kicker is that they are under constant scrutiny by you long before someone else scrutinized them.

The key to understanding why we take ourselves into turmoil lies within our belief regarding our humanity. How many times have you heard people say, "I made that mistake and I am only human?" I have heard it said many times. Being human has become a crutch for some, keeping them grounded and unable to ascend. Living in the space of humanity means I trust my emotions regarding myself, whether good or bad. The danger in that is that the bad seems to overcome the good, especially if you think bad thoughts more than good about yourself. At some point you will need to shift your thinking to what is good and grand in your life. When that shift occurs, it will be then that you will be well able to use your humanity to aid in your ascension. The way you shift your thinking is by becoming aware of every thought that hits you. If it is a debilitating thought, you need to replace it with a life-giving thought. It is just that simple. As you practice living from the place of the spirit and not your humanity, ascension occurs. You will find yourself breaking through glass ceilings, being at a place of unspeakable peace, relaxed even when things at the time are not going as planned. You go beyond that threshold that had you stuck and you peer into what is best for you. You RISE! Ascension requires that you don't ignore what you are feeling, but that you rise to the place of being whole and buoyant.

Spiritually to flow unrestricted in the Kingdom age requires freedom. The Kingdom age is a time of unity and supernatural display of power. A time of multicultural oneness. It is a time where spiritual authority will be positioned in government, education, media, arts and entertainment, etc. As I rose for the Kingdom age, I understood that this freedom was needed for me to hear the Holy Spirit and to act on the instructions. I and you are being positioned beyond the walls of the church to make a difference locally, regionally, nationally, and internationally. We need the liberty to confidently be ourselves, to stand in our truth and be authentic. I had to separate my Spiritual self from my human self. It caused me to be fortified in my Spiritual gifts. It manifested the author, teacher, leader, culture influencer, and entrepreneur in me.

PROPHETIC DECREE: YOU ARE FREE FROM THE GRIPS OF YOUR HUMANITY, YOU ARE FLOWING FREELY IN YOUR SPIRITUAL POWER, AND YOU ARE FLOWING STRATEGICALLY IN THE AREAS YOU ARE PLACED.

CHAPTER 3

PRINCIPLE THREE: THE SCIENCE OF GOD

Most of us wouldn't normally put science and God together. Allow me to tell you that GOD IS SCIENCE! When we look at the creation of the mountains, the oceans, rivers, and trees, we understand that it took supernatural intervention for this to manifest. If we even look at our human anatomy, we can recognize supernatural intervention. Our eyes blink automatically, we breathe automatically, blood flows throughout our body without us flipping a switch. Our organs work automatically without us flipping a switch. So, not only is science God, but GOD IS SCIENCE.

I can recall an instance when I witnessed my first miracle. A powerful female Apostle in Rocky Mount, NC began to pray for a gentleman who was born deaf and dumb. The gentleman was in his mid 40s and was brought to this supernatural service by his mother well into her 60s. As she prayed for him, you could feel the power of the Holy Spirit. She then asked him to say one word and that was "baby". He opened his mouth and said "baby!" The congregation erupted in exuberant praise! I saw a prayer of a spirit-filled individual defy what the doctors said couldn't be done.

I had always been fascinated with miracles and signs of the supernatural. I didn't understand why I felt such calm when I would walk on a trail or in a park where nature was all around. I found that the feeling I had with miracles and signs was the same feeling I had when I walked in nature. I couldn't understand that because I saw them as two different things.

I began to read books from scientists who were finally able to say that God did exist. Well, they didn't quite call it God or Yahweh; they would call it Higher Power or infinite intelligence. One particular scientist had my full attention. Gregg Braden is a best-selling author and scientist. He authored New York Times best sellers The Divine Matrix and Resilience from the Heart. I purchased his book, Human by Design. It was eye-opening to say the least. I was also fascinated with videos regarding his thoughts on the heart connection. He was on to something that spiritual people had always known. There was a direct connection with emotions, feelings, waves of current, healing for the body, and existence outside of our human shell. He had story after story of science and the supernatural having a sort of oneness. It took science to explain what was happening on the inside but it was the supernatural that was manifesting it; they had a cohesive covenant.

My interest was then piqued. I was scrolling through my Netflix one Friday night and a documentary entitled HEAL jumped out at me. I wondered what it was about and sure enough there was more on science and energy healing. It had story after story of emotional healing by energy healers. They were able to identify the trauma and manipulate energy centers in the body to bring healing. Now, those of the more traditional spiritual arenas scoff at things such as these because in their minds they separate this type of healing from the healing received in a church or when someone receives prayer.

When it was all said and done, science had proved that the power to heal could be generated and not from a negative source. It came from a pure source some call Source, Infinite Intelligence, God, Yahweh, Yeshua, or Holy Spirit. I call Him the Holy Spirit. I realized in watching that documentary that the science of God can not be separated from the spirituality of God. GOD IS SCIENCE. One by one, different scientists who were not necessarily religious or spiritual gave accounts of healing.

Now, I know that works with what some of you have been taught, especially in the church arenas. Can we just open our minds to the fact that the Holy Spirit wants to express Himself in many ways? If a person is not exposed to the teachings regarding the Holy Spirit and they experience a miracle or supernatural healing, what do they call the force that did it? That is something to think about. There can be judgement toward those that don't call the Holy Spirit by His name but have they been exposed to the name?

When I looked at the documentary, even in comparison to Gregg Braden, thoughts about it all came back to one thing: SCIENCE AND SPIRITUALITY are one. You can't have creation without Yahweh or as some would call it infinite intelligence. Healings are miracles. When a doctor says there is nothing we can do, then the Holy Spirit heals the individual, it was the science that showed them their hands were tied. It was CAT scans and MRI scans and PET scans that revealed this was beyond their book knowledge.

I recall many occasions where I saw the hand of the Holy Spirit bring miraculous healing. Three particular instances stand out. My oldest aunt lay on lay support in Beaufort, SC. It didn't look good at all. The doctors had given upon her and when they tried to see if she could come off life support, it was an epic fail. She couldn't breathe on her own. So, about six of us, all believers in the healing power of the Holy Spirit, went to Beaufort to pray for our loved one. We went into the ICU two by two to pray for her total healing and recovery. She also had church members doing around the clock prayer for her during that time. We didn't stop praying until we saw the miracle and INDEED WE DID. Within 48 hours she was off the life support, breathing on her own. Within 72 hours she was discharged HOME from the hospital. We knew that if we BELIEVED, ALL THINGS WERE POSSIBLE. We would see her raised up and fully recovered. She is back in her home living alone as I write this. The Healing prayers were heard and the miracle was performed.

The second instance of the power of the Holy Spirit was when

I was notified that a friend of mine's mother was in ICU. There was nothing else the doctors could do and again I went with my friend and we gathered to prayer. The Holy Spirit touched her body and she went home two to three days after. She skipped rehab altogether. Literally from death to LIFE!

I fully understand the covenant that science has with spirituality. I fully embrace both sides of the coin. It is impossible to have one without the other and a miracle can not be performed without participation of both parties.

PROPHETIC DECREE: YOU WILL FULLY EMBRACE AND EXPECT SCIENTIFIC PROOF OF GOD ON EARTH.

CHAPTER 4

PRINCIPLE FOUR: SCIENCE AND SPIRITUALITY

When I think about the Garden of Eden, the first word that comes to mind is COVENANT! Adam and Eve were in covenant with Yahweh. There was a oneness, a cohesiveness, a togetherness, the two were one. They were not only one with each other, but they were one with Yahweh.

Science and Spirituality share the same collaboration. Many would like to separate the two, but in reality they are much like two separate functions that achieve a greater purpose. When I take a walk outside, I can see that the flowers, trees, and birds are flowing freely. Science proves their creation and Spirituality proves there is a Creator. The covenant that is shared between the two is not one that can experience divorce or separation. So, why do scientists and those that are spiritual tend to bump heads about obvious truth? Let's explore some explanations.

Explanation one: Some scientists, physicists, astronomers, and physicians embrace atheism and credit science for our entire creation.

Stephen Hawking, theoretical physicist and atheist stated:

"Spontaneous creation is the reason there is something rather than nothing, why the universe exists, why we exist," he wrote in *The Grand Design*. "It is not necessary to invoke God to light the blue touch paper and set the universe going."

Even on his death bed he didn't feel the need to acknowledge Yahweh as the Creator. He gave credence to science. His belief in the Big Bang Theory was foundational in his life-long set of beliefs that everything had an explanation, but Yahweh wasn't it.

Carl Sagan, an astronomer, stated:

"Science is not only compatible with spirituality; it is the profound source of spirituality."

Every person that was adapted in science was not engulfed in atheism. Francis Collins, who is the director of National Institutes on Health coined this statement that is by far my favorite:

"The God of the bible is also the God of the genome. God can be found in the cathedral or the laboratory."

Dr. Joe Dispenza is an expert in the mind, body, and heart connection. He has connected neuroscience, epigenetics, and quantum physics. He states that: "Science is the contemporary language of mysticism. Become conscious of your unconscious self and the next question is 'what is the greater ideal of who you want to be?'"

Dr. Dispenza can speak about this connection and how the body, heart, and mind connection through meditation brought healing to paralysis in his body. One thought led him into this process: "The power that made the body, heals the body." After a traumatizing bike accident, he was left paralyzed from a spinal injury. He was told he would never walk again. He was able to set intent to focus on what he desired and his body manifested healing within 10 weeks. He is an international speaker and teacher, helping others to be empowered in the same way.

Explanation two: lack of desire to find evidence of God

Many in the scientific fields are simply not open to the idea that Yahweh could have possibly done all the creating, BUT they can't explain why our eyes blink, hearts beat, blood flows through our bodies, and why we have trillions of cells working in symphony. They can put slides under a microscope and can break down what is present in the genome, but refuse to open up to the idea that there is a source from which the genome is created. By the way, a genome is a complete set of genes or genetic material present in a cell or organism.

The Holy Spirit proves on a daily basis that science and spirituality are in covenant. Whenever there is a supernatural occurrence, that is spirituality and science strutting like a peacock. Science explains why a person is paralyzed, spirituality explains the supernatural healing when the person walks again. There is a direct connection between aligning spiritually and healing naturally.

You can read case after case of healing or studies on supernatural occurrences. People will say things like: "I saw a white light" and "I was lifted out of my burning car placed on the other side of the road." There is no scientific way they could have gotten there without some sort of supernatural intervention.

Allow me to share an occurrence that is closer to me than I care to admit. I was in morning-prayer on a Monday and felt an overwhelming sense that something was wrong. I prayed even more earnestly, even though the Spirit had not revealed what was happening. When I came out of prayer, my phone rang and it was my sister. She stated that our mother had been in a head on collision and was at the hospital. I immediately drove about 45 minutes to Rex Hospital in Raleigh. I walked into the room and there was my mother, neck brace on, no glasses, swollen, and clearly uncomfortable. Her car had hydroplaned and the accident took place. Her neck was broken but she was able to walk and talk, but in much pain.

She began to describe the accident and there was a part missing. She remembered hydroplaning but she had no idea how she got to the back seat of her Lincoln. When the paramedics arrived she was in the back seat with her seatbelt still buckled in the driver's seat. Now, you can put a spin on it any way you would like, but we knew that an Angelic presence moved her from the front to the back because I believe the direct impact would have killed her on the spot.

When I took her to the car, she cried. She couldn't believe she had survived when she looked at the mangled wreck. We have always been believers of Yahweh's hand of protection but we now had another example of that supernatural power. Science showed her which vertebras in her neck were broken, but spirituality gave reason for her life. I mean, how else can you explain a full grown woman laying flat on her back in the backseat of the car with the front seatbelt still fastened? Again, it took the covenant of them both to bring clarity to the entire story. One without the other would have left big gaps in the story.

That may not have convinced you that science and spirituality are doing a dance. They dance every day, explaining and recording. For the things that are mysterious to the atheist, are supernatural to the believer. The Gospel of Mark 9:23 (KJV) records, "If thou canst believe all things are possible to him that believeth." That is good enough for me because I have experience with the Holy Spirit's mighty acts. I never have had to put the Holy Spirit to a test, He does what the third person of the triune Godhead was sent to do— BRING COMFORT! Yeshua told the disciples in John 14:16(KJV), "And I will pray the Father, and He shall give you another comforter, that he may abide with you forever."

Science and Spirituality are in covenant and that covenant will never be broken; they are one.

PROPHETIC DECREE: YOU WILL EMBRACE THE SCIENCE AND SPIRITUALITY OF GOD AND GAIN GREATER UNDERSTANDING OF THE SPIRIT REALM.

CHAPTER 5

PART II - 12 PRINCIPLES OF ASCENSION

PRINCIPLE FIVE: ALIGNMENT

I am an early morning riser. I have been since I was young. When I began daily meditation in 2016 I loved being able to start my day in the right frame of mind. Meditation was clear in the Scripture. I was to meditate on His word, day and night Joshua 1:8 (KJV). I understood that meditation was not just praying to something outside of me, but that it connected me with the Holy Spirit internally. The Spirit never left me, I didn't have to wait until Wednesday night Bible study or Sunday morning service to meet the presence of Yahweh. He was always there.

As I began to align or, better explained, come into agreement with who the Holy Spirit revealed to me I was, my life began to change. I began to shift my eating habits. I couldn't understand it, but I began to desire more organic foods. I didn't do away with the buffet visits (LOL), but I observed an 80/20 rule. I introduced intermittent fasting later on but I began with just changes in diet. I was prompted to do this after I asked the Holy Spirit about healing for a heart defect I was born with. I had mitral valve prolapse. My first diagnosis of the defect was around 15. It didn't necessarily bother me but I didn't like the fact that I had to have a cardiologist, yearly visits, and yearly echocardiograms when I wasn't elderly.

The Spirit instructed me first regarding diet, then exercise, along with my meditation. I also was taking a BP pill, a water pill to be exact. I wanted to be free from medication and the defect. I knew that my body could heal itself when I shifted the environment for healing. Well, it wasn't long before the results came pouring in. Not only was my heart defect healed, but my BP came down so much, my physician had to take me off the BP meds. What I focused on during that time was the total healing of body and heart. I opened myself to more love, released the pain of the past, and found myself in a better mental space. I lived in the present moment, stayed away from politics and anything that would unravel me. I was calmer and everything was lighter. I didn't speed as much, rushing from one thing to another. I WAS FULLY ALIGNED with who I had always been. I was fully conscious, fully healed, fully relaxed, and fully trusting...you could say I WAS WOKE!

Another key I found that assisted me in alignment was opening my heart to unconditional love. This is the mind-heart-body connection that Dr. Dispenza speaks about. Through the use of meditation on who I am, not what I want to become. Now, when you meditate, your mind and body will assume you are already there, not that you are on your way. So, as I opened my heart more and more, I had clear, healthy boundaries in relationships, I saw people for who they are, not for what I wanted them to be, I practiced acceptance instead of forcing changes, I loved myself more, saw myself as a Spirit Being, not just a human being. It made me overall an attractor of love, peace, joy, and the list goes on.

If you read in Galatians 5:22-23(KJV), you will see some of these same characteristics. There are nine fruits of the Holy Spirit, distinct characteristics, and when I aligned I had access to all nine. I was indeed spiritually tuned to who I was outside of this flesh suit. I wasn't just another religious fanatic, super spiritual mystic, or charismatic voice. I was indeed flowing in THE SUPERNATURAL ME.

ALIGNMENT + THE SUPERNATURAL = MIRACLES, SIGNS AND WONDERS

As I moved more into daily meditation I began to teach others the benefits of aligning in meditation. What I learned was that meditation was not just something done by those in eastern religions. It was a western religious philosophy that had moved us away from connecting to the source of power. It moved us away from infinite intelligence and caused us to depend on a God outside of us not inside. In all actuality we had created another God that we were praying to inside, becoming aware of the Holy Spirit that was on the inside. When I got the revelation that God was in me, not outside of me, my POWER OPENED UP. It was like I no longer relied on what anyone told me, I began to be a seeker of what the truth was. I found it and it wasn't far off from the way I had been taught.

My Christian upbringing gave me a sure foundation that I could build on. I just knew there was more to it than just gathering for church, reading scriptures, and following rules and regulations. When I opened my awareness to receive the baptism of the Holy Spirit, it made me a believer. All at once I was living in the Book of Acts Chapter 2. I was having my own Pentecostal experience with the evidence of speaking in tongues. Now, many are skeptical about this supernatural occurrence; I am just not one of those skeptics. I recognized that when I began to tap into what was already available for me, there was a direct manifestation of the supernatural.

There are many religions, many of which have been created by followers of the Teacher that coined the scripture. Jesus' followers who study the Bible are called disciples or Christians. I personally think there is a difference between the two, but I will expound on that later. Buddhists follow the teachings of Buddha in the Eight Fold Path. Muslims study the Quran and are followers of their Teacher, Muhammad, and Allah, which means god. Now, I am not here to debate any religion; you have a free will, I can only speak most fluently on my own path of spirituality as a disciple of Jesus Christ.

You see, I am not just a Christian or a person that follows Christianity. Christianity is the religion. I am free from religion and I embraced discipleship because it gave me a way of life. It wasn't just a set of rules and rituals; it was a way of living day to day. It was a living where I could display Christ's grace and compassion to all. Whatever be your choice, you will have to come into alignment with what that Teacher teaches. Many in the church arena may not agree with that statement, but I am the author of this book. We can't take away a person's free will by making them select a spiritual path that is most comfortable for us. Ultimately, alignment is up to the individual; there is no such thing as dictatorship when it comes to the Holy Spirit. He is not tyrannical, contrary to what is taught in many pulpits across America.

Once I aligned to who I knew I was, studying the Words of Yahweh from the Hebraic understanding, I was able to do the things that my teacher did. I was able to perform miracles, I was able to see signs and wonders demonstrated. These signs shall follow them that believe…that portion of Scripture was my mantra for many years. I wanted to see the supernatural. I wanted to view the supernatural happening in others. I wanted to watch others heal and I wanted to see my own body healed in the areas where dis-ease was present.

ALIGN with the limitless, boundless you. ALIGN with who you are outside of this human body and watch the SUPERNATURAL flow endlessly through you.

PROPHETIC DECREE: YOU ARE ALIGNING WITH WHO YOU WERE AT THE BEGINNING, THAT YOU ARE BECOMING AWARE OF YOUR SUPERNATURAL POWER WITH UNLIMITED ACCESS.

CHAPTER 6

PRINCIPLE SIX: ASSIGNMENT

In seventh grade I would enter my math class with Mr. Collins and our homework assignment would be on the chalkboard. We would come in and sit down and write down that assignment. It was understood that it had to be completed; there were no ifs, ands, or buts about it. Mr. Collins was not taking any excuses; the next morning our assignment was to be turned in or we would receive a zero.

Our life assignments are much like that. It is as easy as that assignment written on that board and the person responsible if it doesn't get done, it's totally your fault.

Every walking, talking individual has a purpose on earth. For instance, I am fully aware that one of my purposes is to bring healing to earth with all my gifts. Whether I am teaching, training, vacationing, enjoying family, creating wealth, or traveling, I bring healing. I am able to bring healing in all arenas—not just the one I was reared in. So that assignment has required me to open my mind to teachers and philosophies that I would have never engaged in. I am not satisfied with mediocrity. I have a need to be well-rounded, have the ability to speak on different subjects and understand what it really takes to ascend to a higher level of supernatural flow. I had to choose to live from my heart and access the fully-conscious me. My assignment required me to heal perpetually. Life was going to continue to happen and I would have to make the choice to keep recreating the life I desire. I had to choose the life I wanted and not get stuck in the traumas of the past. I had to allow myself to let go of the things that block my growth. I had to relieve myself of the unconscious programs that I picked up along my journey. I had to accept my past and move in the present so that my future would be different from my past. This is what assignment presses you to do. It causes you to manifest from your heart.

TRAUMA AND BROKENNESS

Unearthing trauma caused me to have to revisit my divorce. I can not even explain how devastated I was at this event. This single event had the ability to change my course of life from abundance to lacking. I had only just begun to live as a mother, as a wife, and as an emerging leader. The chain of events that happened after that divorce refined, pruned, and fashioned me. I knew every day that I didn't want to live in this place of depression and defeat for the rest of my life, fighting back suicidal thoughts and barely keeping my head above water. My assignment to heal others was still there during that time, even though I was going through one of the harshest trials I could endure. I didn't realize how much healing I would have to experience to be well-versed in how to walk through trauma and brokenness and not reside there.

It took a few trips to my therapist for talk therapy to get me back on track with my assignment. She let me sit, cry, and share my harrowing story. She never interrupted and it seemed like each season unearthed something deeper within me. I had suppressed so much from childhood on. She became a trauma archeologist, unearthing those deep-seated feelings and opening the compartments within me that had been locked away. The greatest lesson I learned from her is that I was NOT MY PAST. I was NOT MY TRAUMA. I was NOT MY BROKENNESS. In all actuality, I was not what had happened to me or how I felt about it. I had all the potential within to change the course and complete my destiny. I began to take baby steps and each year things got better. I finished school and received my Business Administration Degree, a better job literally dropped in my lap, and life was taking great turns. I was still experiencing disappointments, I still had to contend with those that hindered my work, but that was life. I had to accept that life was going to happen no matter how many great things are handed to you. There will be good with bad and there will be tears and joy. My assignment is still there and so is my purpose.

I saw this in an amazing display while watching a movie on Netflix. The movie was entitled Holiday in the Inn. It was a movie about a woman who was a newlyminted empty-nester and whose husband decided he was no longer in love and he was moving out. She had planned this amazing trip for them to reconnect and ended up going without him. That one trip changed the course of her life. She reconnected with her purpose. She loved animals and had the opportunity to work at an elephant reserve. Not only did she reconnect with her purpose, but she found love and wasn't even looking for it. Her assignment and purpose never changed, even though she was married to someone who really didn't care for animals the way that she did. His walking out on the marriage allowed her to restore what was needed in her to regain footing in her purpose.

There are times when someone will walk out of your life only to make room for the purpose you are destined for. They served as a distraction and as you move in your assignment, it requires having all hands on deck. In other words, there can't be hindrances to your work. There can't be those that are just hanging out in your life to reap benefits, but not be pivotal in pushing you to the next dimension. There will be times when someone will be led out of your life in one season, only to be brought back in another one. The key is not to reach back to usher them back in until they have gone through the channels needed to exist in your life in a healthy way. A toxic, inconsistent friendship or relationship will only be a hindrance to your assignment. You need mental clarity, not competition. You will love, not hate; you need someone to know what you are capable of doing and who understands you are on a journey and support is needed.

Your assignment is great, but it will be up to you to complete it. Your purpose is needed, but it will be up to you to fulfill it.

You are here to be blessed and be a blessing, but it's up to you to exist in both phases.

PROPHETIC DECREE: YOU HAVE FULLY EMBRACED YOUR ASSIGNMENT AND ALL HINDERANCES HAVE BEEN REMOVED THAT WOULD PREVENT YOU FROM MOVING FORWARD IN A HEALTHY WAY.

CHAPTER 7

PRINCIPLE SEVEN: ALLOWING

I recall the first time I heard a talk done by Esther Hicks of Abraham Hicks Publications. As an avid learner, I was intrigued and at the same time open to gain greater understanding. Esther is an author of several books, two of which I have: *The Vortex* and *Ask and It shall Be Given*. She taught people for over 20 years to tap into the pure conscious part of them through meditation and as creators to be the captains of their destiny. This is actually the same thing that is taught in ministries all over the world. The book of Matthew records the Scripture: Ask and it shall be given to you, seek and ye shall find and knock and the door shall be open. Well, it doesn't take a rocket scientist to figure out these are the same principles. I tuned into one of her teachings on my lunch break one day and heard her use a term. Her workshops used to be called the Science of Deliberate Creation. She renamed them the ART OF ALLOWING. The premise was that if we could focus on allowing, instead of creating tedious work, the manifestation of desires would be easier.

Well, my background gives the same path through faith. When I relax that things are already done and focus on the outcome, I see the manifestation of what I believe. Hebrews 11:1(KJV) records: Now faith is the substance of things hoped for and the evidence of things not seen. Yes, they both are the same. If we make a comparison, we see not only similarity, but identical principles. So, what does it really take to allow?

In some Christian circles, meditation is taboo. It is seen as an eastern religion thing and western religion just doesn't have room for it. Well, that notion is easily disputed by one of several scriptures in the Bible regarding meditation. Joshua 1:8(KJV) records: Meditate on His word day and night. So meditation is a tool that should be used, no matter what your spiritual path.

I described the differences between meditation and prayer in one of my two monthly teachings. I explained that prayer is talking to someone outside of you, while meditation is focusing on the supernatural power within. It causes you to see what you desire and see it as your normal. There are different types of prayers and ultimately they all direct you to something outside of yourself. God is not on the outside of us, even though He is manifested through nature and the universe itself. He is a conscious, ever-present, always in motion spirit that governs our existence from the inside out. He is not a forceful spirit. When you allow, He expands within and causes you to see what is possible.

As we have heard from generations of teachers, we have become dulled in our senses regarding our supernatural abilities. We have been taught we need permission from someone to flow in the power of Creation. What's funny is we didn't come here getting permission from any person. We were manifested on earth by the creative power of the universe. The Holy Spirit or what some of you would call source energy marvelously sculpted our beings and now we are here. The earth is matter, not spirit. We are flanked in an earth-suit to be able to maintain while on this earth journey. We all have a distinct purpose for why we are here and we are not just passing through. It is necessary to connect with our original purpose, in order to live fully.

I don't care for wasting time, I am a person that likes to be productive unless I am just having a lazy day. Walking this earthly journey, not flowing in purpose is literally equivalent to wasting time. Time that you didn't create. Time that you have no control over. It is up to you to allow or disallow. You disallow by not knowing who you are and by being a chameleon to all those around you. Do you know what a chameleon does? They become like the environment where they are to hide. It is a mechanism that keeps them from being in plain view of danger.

As human beings, when you take on these characteristics, you mold into the people you are around. You mold into the opinions you are around. You mold into the destinies you are around. You hide who you really are because you really don't believe in yourself. Deep down there is a disconnect with the original design. You are created to be of value in the earth realm. You were created in a singular form to help you to see that your fingerprints are not the same as those around you. Even identical twins have different fingerprints. They may be identical in looks to those that see them, but to their mother or father they are two different individuals. There is a feature that is different to tell them apart; that one feature gives them uniqueness.

What is your one feature that gives you uniqueness? What is the ability that you have that no one else has? If you allow those Spirit-given abilities to come forth, you will see how easy it is to flow in who you are. After all, you will always do a terrible job at trying to be someone else.

Coco Chanel quoted some powerful words when she said: "In order to be irreplaceable one must remain different." This was her response regarding her never marrying. She had built an empire on authenticity and unique ability. She wasn't an imposter. She never hid behind another's image. She knew doors would open for her based on the value she had, not on someone else's ability to open them. It is a different line of thinking when you know WHO YOU ARE. Who you are now is who you have evolved into based on life experiences, gifts, goals, traumas, disappointments, and joys. Just as a baby evolves from a newborn into a grown man. The same goes for you as you ascend on earth. You are here to learn and grow. You are here to remember who you are based on your original design. You came with your own fingerprints, your own DNA, and it is not duplicated in another. If you allow yourself to JUST BE, you will be amazed at how you blossom. The caterpillar is only in the cocoon for a short span of time and out comes the butterfly. If you understand that principle, you would know that, just as that caterpillar needed to evolve to see higher heights, so do you. Flying gives you a different view than crawling on the ground. NOW LET THAT MARINATE!

PROPHETIC DECREE: YOU HAVE MOVED INTO AN ERA OF ALLOWING. ALLOWING YOUR GIFTS TO SHINE AND THEY ARE NOW MAKING ROOM FOR YOU.

CHAPTER 8

PRINCIPLE EIGHT: AUTHENTICITY

One Saturday morning I was reading a news article online about how store owners were arrested for selling knock off clothing and bags. Well, for some reason the article caught my attention. I have read other articles before but I decided to dig into the details. There was an undercover sting operation and the authorities had been watching these stores and store owners for sometime. They spent their time gathering evidence, and at that point they were able to make an arrest. Though the value of the products sold was in the thousands, the value of the original products was IN THE MILLIONS. They were charged not based on the value of the knock offs, but of the authentic products.

You are an original. I know you have heard that before, so let me give you my definition of what an original is. An original is a product, service, or person that can not be duplicated because of their extremely high value and authenticity. It didn't matter that the knock off products had the brand name on them, they were still knock offs. The originality was missing and the authorities could clearly pick out the fakes. THAT'S HOW YOU ARE! Whatever you have to offer is authentic; it's really real. No one has the capacity to repackage it because you DIED FOR IT. You had to walk a certain road to do what you do. You had to do without certain things, watch people walk away, run with imposters, deal with the loneliness of the call, and even deal with feelings of being burdened even though God said you were blessed. See, everyone wants to ride in on the glory but no one wants to live your story.

Your story is your fingerprint. It is your unique characteristic of what sets you apart. It is the way that you are able to flow unhindered. No one walks like you, talks like you, brings value like you do. It is your authenticity. So, if we all are authentic, what prevents us from walking fully in it? There are several reasons, but let's explore two.

REASON #1: FEAR

When you are afraid to move, you have no other choice but to stand still. You can know you are different, but you fear the risk it takes in moving. When my grandson Kingsley was learning to walk, he would be hesitant and fearful. He would grip his dad's hand for dear life, refusing to let him go. Even when his dad would try to let him go on his own, I would see him reach up with his other hand and hold onto him with both. He had legs to walk, but fear in his heart. It wasn't about ability; he had strong legs. It was about the fear in his mind that he was not steady enough to walk. Well, of course now HE RUNS (LOL). It didn't take him long to get accustomed to walking, but he didn't get it until FEAR LEFT.

REASON #2: YOU WEREN'T TAUGHT TO VALUE YOURSELF

Many of us were taught to move but not taught our value. Back to my grandson—we would say to him, "Kingsley, you have strong legs, you can walk." We would tell him he could do it. We added value to his ability. When we are not taught to value ourselves, it is difficult to flow authentically. Many of us have learned our value on our own. Then, when we realized our value, we were able to align with others that gave us that push. It is imperative that you are around people that give you the push that is needed to know your value. There have to be reminders along the way because things will get off kilter. Some days you may not feel authentic and your circle is then able to say, "It doesn't look like it, BUT YOU STILL ARE VALUABLE."

When we can harness our unmatched value, something in us opens up. Authenticity on another level shines forth. You stretch yourself, expand yourself, and are consistent in growth and development. Nothing stops you. You go from being stopped over every little thing, to evolving into this SUDDENLY UNSTOPPABLE MACHINE! You bulldoze your way through, knowing that you are creating the life you dreamed about. AUTHENTICITY IS A MUST IN ASCENSION.

PROPHETIC DECREE: YOU ARE NOW EMBRACING YOUR AUTHENTIC SELF, YOUR VALUE IS BEING SEEN AND HEARD, DOORS ARE OPEN BECAUSE OF YOUR AUTHENTIC NATURE AND YOUR ABILITY TO DO WHAT NO ONE ELSE CAN.

CHAPTER 9

PART III - 12 PRINCIPLES OF ASCENSION

PRINCIPLE NINE: LAW OF ATTRACTION AND LAW OF FAITH

I know you have heard of the Law of Attraction. It is the one of the spiritual laws that governs our universe. The Law of Attraction states that similar energies are drawn together by the magnetic power of their similarities. Literally it is "like attracts like." The Law of Faith, is the belief that what you have hoped for, will produce evidence . Your mind and belief in something will draw it to you. These two laws are virtually the same. One is measured by science, the other is measured by spirituality.

It will require FAITH to ascend in mind that your environment matches what you think. I was listening to Bishop TD Jakes earlier one morning. He is one of my favorite teachers of the Gospel. He said there are times when your apparel doesn't match where you are going but God will clothe you so that your environment changes in accordance with what you believe you are destined to be. That was profound. What he explained is, if I believe my destiny is bigger than what I am right now, I will draw that destiny to me. I may not have the resources, I may not have the knowledge of how to flow in that space, I may not have the connections, but MY FAITH in where I am going DRAWS THE DOORS OPEN. As I walk through the doors, the Holy Spirit gives me the knowledge to maintain myself in the place I have walked into. Literally it's like getting a job you have never done, with no degree, no background, no influences— JUST BELIEF.

Let's take this a step further. I will share a transparent moment with you. When I was growing up, I was able to get a work permit at 14. Before I turned 14, when my mother would take me with her to the grocery store, I would think to myself, "I want my first job to be a grocery bagger." Well, I just held that thought and sure enough when I turned 14, my first job I landed was a grocery bagger. I thought about it so much, I literally manifested it through my belief that I already saw myself doing. My entire life has been that way. Every job I worked, when I purchased cars or my home, I already saw it long before I did it. I didn't know it then, but I was always being prepared for my *next* with all the things I went through. Each blessing had attached to it a process. So I had to submit to the process of what it would take to get me into those places.

As an author, teacher, businesswoman, and apostolic teacher, I haven't always worked for myself. I haven't always had rental properties. I haven't always had multiple streams of income. I haven't always been able to relocate to the city I desired. I do all these things now, but I saw it long before I did it. 2020 has been the most pivotal and transitional year in my life. I have connected with great influencers, I have stood to teach on platforms that I only saw in the Spirit. I have increased in my business and continue to add more businesses. I have always seen myself as an ENTERPRISE. I wanted to be the first to do things that no one had done in my family and lead my sons into that legacy. My taking the leap into those things has set a course for a new path for my sons and grandchildren. They never have to see the struggle that I endured as a single parent. Though we struggled, they learned the meaning of divine favor. God took care of us. We always had a roof over our heads and we always had food to eat. We always had someone willing to help. They were what I called my years of famine that led me into my years of plentitude.

These laws, whichever you choose to use, will be vital in your ascension. If you don't believe you are going somewhere, you will never get there. You have to literally place yourself in that spot. You have to walk through the scenes of your destiny. You have to see it before you tangibly have it. You have to know that you belong in those scenes. You have to know that the scene is incomplete without you in it. If you believe that you have stepped in that divine plan, it is now necessary for you to BE IT, not just talk about it.

One of the things that has hurt us on our spiritual journeys is that we haven't always been taught to walk through it, we have been taught to just pray for it. We haven't realized that we made the petition but didn't walk in a place of dominion. Our dominion was given to us in the book of Genesis. That means by virtue of your dominion, you can decree and declare what you have seen and the power of that belief will magnetize that to you. These daily declarations, meditations, and affirmations are necessary for ascension to greater levels.

Let's talk about the power of meditation combined with the Law of Faith. For those that are ascribed to the more western religions, there is a tendency to classify meditation as new age. However, throughout the Bible there is supporting evidence of meditation. Psalm 77:12(KJV), Psalm 63:6(KJV), Joshua 1:8(KJV), and Philippians 4:8-9(Message) are just a few of those passages. While I love the book of Joshua, I lean more towards the Philippians passage…

Philippians 4:8-9 The Message (MSG)
"Summing it all up, friends, I'd say you'll do best by filling your minds and meditating on things true, noble, reputable, authentic, compelling, gracious—the best, not the worst; the beautiful, not the ugly; things to praise, not things to curse. Put into practice what you learned from me, what you heard and saw and realized. Do that, and God, who makes everything work together, will work you into his most excellent harmonies."

The instruction here is to meditate on what you know is TRUTH! All the things that are true for you and true for your destiny, ponder these things. You can't help but to produce harmony when you lean toward what is TRUTH.

Whether you call it Law of Faith or Law of Attraction, you are working by the same principles. Be open to the synonymous nature of the two. You don't have to debate what words to call it, you just need to put to practice the principle. All of Creation is governed by spiritual laws. Those laws are irrefutable and always working. Now, whether they work for your good or for your bad, is up to you. It is according to what truth you meditate and think on.

PROPHETIC DECREE: I DECREE AND DECLARE THAT YOU WILL BE COMPELLED TO MEDITATE ON THE TRUTH OF WHO YOU ARE, THE ABILITIES THAT YOU HOLD, AND THE LIMITLESS NATURE OF YOUR SUCCESS.

CHAPTER 10

PRINCIPLE TEN: EVOLUTION

Scientists have their own definition of evolution. They have their own theory regarding how the world came to be. While I have a healthy respect for science because you can't separate it from God, evolution is a subject where we disagree. I figure that is ok to do so because we all are entitled to have our own beliefs and reservations regarding theories. I believe in the Creation of the world by Yahweh. I do not believe we evolved from apes or any other animal. I believe we were created human beings with high-level intelligence over every other being. I don't believe in the Big Bang Theory as a truth. I believe that the world was in the strategic plan of Yahweh and that what we see is handiwork of creative supernatural power. Let's take evolution a step further.

To evolve in my own words means to grow from one state to another. This could be mentally, emotionally, or physically. Children evolve from toddlers to teens. Teens evolve into adults. At some point the physical body stops growing taller and we begin to evolve more inwardly. Growth can be measured by years but it is easy for a 90-year-old to look 60 because of the lifestyle of healthy living. So, whereas they are not growing physically, they are maintaining wellness by preserving the body they have. You can evolve emotionally after having dealt with marked trauma and move into a healthier emotional state. As spiritual beings, we are always in motion. Our thoughts can govern our evolution to our benefit.

This year I begin a series of workshops addressing evolution of the mind. I entitled them HEAL2020. I would take a group of students and first pinpoint the potential dangers when we don't evolve. Living in the past is a choice and you have to choose to live beyond it. I then would show them how one traumatic event as a child growing up can evolve into bigger emotional hang-ups as adults. Trauma can evolve into sabotage. Sabotage can evolve into cyclic patterns. Once I laid the groundwork of the cycle, I was able to give them a strategy to evolve past the traumatic event and create a new narrative.

Evolution to ascension requires a new story to be created. Remember now, your narrative is the spoken or written account of the events or stories of your life. If you hold the narrative that people are always using you, you will continue to attract users and manipulators. Remember your thoughts become things, we are creative beings and thinking of it long enough can manifest it in your life. You can change the narrative and what the story represents in your life. For instance, my divorce at 25 after only five years of marriage, for years was a failure to me. I saw it as a space where I failed as a wife and mother. My two sons and I endured years of struggle even though those years were more peaceful than if I had remained married.

When I began to change the narrative into it being an event that needed to take place in my life, I needed to uproot the need to be accepted, to be seen, to be heard, and to be understood. Part of my reason for marrying was not for love; it was for acceptance. I needed someone to believe in me. I needed someone to come home to that wouldn't toss me away. Those were all the wrong reasons to marry. I wanted children and it was just expected that marriage would be a part of that. Well, if I'd have been living in the times that we are in now, I would have known that as a single person I could have still mothered children through adoption or foster care.

Formulating a new narrative means that I look at my event as a catalyst for growth, not an obstacle to my ascension. I had to look at my years of financial struggle as a time for me to learn to trust Yahweh in me even the more. I had to see the things that my sons and I experienced along the way and that generated a breaking ground for the latter years of abundance, wealth, and success. I had to see my years of depression as a catalyst to push me toward helping others being healed. I experienced physical and mental sickness but I OVERCAME IT ALL when I changed the narrative.

The second step to evolution is maintaining the new narrative. Changing the narrative is painless, maintaining the narrative can be tedious. You have to know something about your brain. Your brain has memory centers that hold all of life's happenings and events. You not only hold memory in your brain but every cell in your body memorizes events, disappointments, reactions, etc. So you have to make an effort to create the new narrative and uproot years of the old one. It is equivalent to learning how to eat better and engage in a healthy lifestyle.

Two years ago I decided to eat healthier and exercise more. Exercise was not a hard thing to implement as I have done sports all my life. I played on several teams and I love being active. What worked against me was my programmed way of eating. I had to shift from vegetable oil to virgin coconut oil. I had to incorporate more raw veggies and fruits. I had to have a balanced diet, not just be active. It required me to become a more conscious consumer. It changed the way I shopped for food, I even desired more organic food than I did before. I learned how to season with organic spices and seasoning. I monitored my sodium intake and carb intake, and drank herbal teas daily. I wasn't on a temporary diet. I wasn't trying to have a temp fix for my body transformation. I wanted something that I could adapt to overtime. I had to MAINTAIN the narrative.

Maintaining the narrative takes discipline. It takes consistently doing the thing that is needed over a period of time. You have to want to evolve more than to remain in your past. Your past should only serve as your point of reference that's for learning. It was never supposed to be the place of residence. When we make a stop at a permanent residence, evolution is difficult to experience.

An additional enemy to evolution of mind, body, and soul is ancient trauma. Traumatic events that have taken their toll on your mind. The trauma you continue to rehearse over and over again. The event that happened long enough ago that you are physically and mentally no longer in that space. Evolution requires you to live in the present moment. Healing is needed to move safely past that. It is now safe to heal the past. It is pertinent to your ascension. Ancient trauma is what I call the trauma that could have possibly matriculated from your childhood or early years of growth. It has been your garment, it has been your talking piece, it has become the abnormality that you are used to. You give it power over you when you refuse to transmute the pain into progress. It is exactly what the rape victim does when they share their story of triumph over their assailant. They take their power back and utilize it to help others heal. Evolution makes you a catalyst for healing.

It doesn't matter what you have endured or will endure from this day forward. There is nothing stopping you from ascending. You have to choose to evolve, you have to choose to release the past, you have to make a decision to forgive and go through the process of healing. EVOLUTION IS A CHOICE and it can be one of the best decisions you will ever make.

PROPHETIC DECREE: YOU WILL EVOLVE AT AN ACCELERATED PACE, YOU WILL RELEASE AT QUANTUM LEAP PROPORTIONS, AND YOU WILL MOVE ASSUREDLY INTO YOUR DESTINY.

CHAPTER 11

PRINCIPLE ELEVEN: CULTURED FOR ASCENSION

We have tunneled through ten vital principles of ascension. These last two principles give you a sneak peek into what life will be like when our society embraces ascension. Ascension will become our culture, our way of life, our way of thinking, doing, and being. The entire earth is going through scientific and spiritual upgrades like you would not believe. We have experienced things such as fires, floods, tsunamis, earthquakes, and even the threat of war. We literally have seen the burning away of old systems. Religious systems have been hit hard. The bondage of religion is being broken down brick by brick. Political and educational systems have been dismantled. It is one of the greatest shifts we have seen in decades. While some are trying to protect the old way of thinking, others are pressing through with new paradigms for the next generation to implement.

It takes time and effort to grow a culture into ascension. It will take those individuals such as yourself, putting on full display your move through your ascension cycle. Much like David was on full display in his battle with Goliath. Many felt he was ill equipped, but David understood that he could only use what he knew would work for him. Ascension is about you KNOWING YOURSELF. You can't afford to have an identity crisis. You have to transition with ease out of the systems-molded mind and body into a spiritually-molded mind and body. You have to know that what you aspire to be, you already are. You are now becoming more aware of who you were at the beginning. This is why life has been about learning and growing.

Once evolution takes place, you are unable to go back to the old you. You literally have reprogrammed yourself so precisely that the old you isn't even appealing. The old you will fight the new you from emerging. It doesn't matter how much the old keeps presenting itself, you keep moving forward. Your appetite for the old way of thinking and moving is gone. It has been burned up in the new thought paradigm. Your ascension impressed in your mind the past only as a reference point. The past is only the place of learning, not the place of repetition. It is the place of growing pains, not chronic pain. Chronic pain is ongoing and never-ending. It doesn't wane, it is intense most of the time. Your past is only intense when you are living it. The intensity leaves when the event is over. Where you feel the intensity is in your mind through the memory.

I recall a season in my life when I had a great loss in a personal relationship. It was one of the lowest times of my life. I had to move on without the one person that I really felt understood me as a person, as a woman, as a leader, and as an influencer. I had to reach down into the deepest part of me and began the grief process. The process seemed tedious and long, and escaping the memories daily was a chore. I would be exhausted and without peace. It didn't matter how much Scripture I read or how many encouraging words I came across. There was this gaping hole in my heart that seemingly couldn't be filled by anyone but this person. Well, I began my times of isolation and in what I thought was loneliness, I began to see from a different perspective. I deliberately isolated myself so that I could finally face the reality that this person was no longer a part of my bigger picture. I had tried to replace and failed miserably. I only made the inevitable more delayed. I had to face it. So after two or three weeks of trying to do the move on and replace strategy, it unraveled. I was again left to my thoughts about this connection.

What I had believed was that this covenant with this person was going to be beneficial to my life-long growth and endeavors. We were best friends and that was what I felt I needed as we moved toward our destinies. We had constant clashes because our brokenness began to show up in our friendship. Our insecurities, fears, anxieties, and woundedness were made front and center. That usually happens with close-knit relationships. Heat tends to bring to the surface the things that are hidden that we just don't want to be vulnerable to. So it ended, and I had a hard time accepting it. After all, we had parted before, but it was only temporarily; we always found a way back to our friendship. We learned lessons and each return back was a better run than the first. This last clash was not like that. I had grown so weary that walking away was easier than it had ever been. I questioned all of my reasons why I even had the friendship. I wanted to classify it as a hindrance but I really couldn't. I was then left with a brokenness of heart that I was clueless on how to fix. This time I needed more than a scripture, I needed an action that would reset my mind and override my memory. It was then that I had an epiphany. I realized at that vital moment that my heart wasn't broken but my narrative was.

Our hearts naturally open to love and acceptance. I had done that when I began the friendship. So my heart was working just fine. However, the story I placed on my open heart was LIFE WILL NOW GO LIKE THIS SINCE THIS PERSON IS HERE. Underneath that scenario was a life where I mostly didn't feel supported. I supported others but didn't always get the same in return. I deeply longed for someone to see not the programmed me but the authentic me—Me IN THE RAW—the me that if you could love her, you would pass the test. I found that with this friend the love we had remained intact with all the ups and downs of friendship. We still wanted the best for each other. We still cheered each other on even when just two days ago we were at each other's throats. Well, between competition, proving, and insecurity we were both TIRED! There was nothing left and I didn't know how my friend was doing because we were in a season of silence. I could only do what I knew to do— REWRITE MY NARRATIVE.

Life had produced this pattern of behavior in me that I wasn't aware of. I would meet people and I would say to myself, "This person would make a great friend," because great friends were few and far between. I would then incorporate them into every area of my life and sometimes they just didn't fit. I always felt like I had to include people in my vision but I later learned that wasn't true. Some people are supporters, some people are hands on. Some will only support from afar and others up close. I had pretty much put everyone in the same category. I had to break the cycle and dug deeper into my tool of meditation to do that.

I began writing and using affirmations that brought out my ability to exist outside of my connections, while still being connected. I began to really focus on the expectations I had of myself, not the people in my life. I learned to let go of the expectations of those people and my narrative began to reformulate. I took myself inward to the place where all answers exist; my relationship with the Holy Spirit. There has never been a time when I had a question and didn't get an answer. While letting go of the pressure I placed on others to be what I desired, I learned that I had to embrace who I knew myself to be. It wasn't their responsibility to just be in my life to be a part of everything I have. They had their own things, they made their own moves. They did what was necessary and needed to create a life they envisioned. I had to take a step back because I also realized I was mature in areas where others were not. My pulling them into my vision was a huge mistake because they didn't have the discipline required to carry out certain tasks. Long story short, I learned more about myself in those times of isolation. It wasn't just one time, it was several times. I had tears and I had joy. I had relief and I had grief. All of the emotions I felt were all for my good. And all of it pushed me not just into a mind of ascension, but I was CULTURED IN ASCENSION.

That one friendship with my best friend catapulted me into this whole new world of ascension homeostasis. I no longer visited ascension, but I LIVED THERE. It was now a part of my culture. It was now a part of my way of life and my existence. I could never go back if I tried. I had elevated in mind, body, and soul so much so that every part of me was different. During that time I ate more raw foods, cutting out the carbs and sugars. I began to align more my eating with ascension. I had always been pretty healthy but this was on a different level. I was participating in my health in a greater way. I had more mental clarity, I had more prophetic visions and dreams. One traumatic event that could have made me bitter PUSHED me in the other direction.

You may feel like you are going through the worst experience ever and it very well may be. But this is the explosion that is needed to destroy old thinking and old ways of doing. After that the bulldozers can come through and clean off the debris, where building something brand new is feasible. OLD THINGS ARE PASSED AWAY. This is YOUR NEW BEGINNING. You will now experience MIRACLES, SIGNS, AND WONDERS on a daily basis. And for that you should be grateful.

PROPHETIC DECREE: YOU WILL NOW LIVE IN A PLACE OF MENTAL AND SPIRITUAL CLARITY, YOU WILL SEE EVERY EVENT AS A LEARNING AND GROWING PROCESS, YOU WILL TEAR DOWN OLD SYSTEMS TO CREATE A NEW WAY OF THINKING IN THIS ASCENDED CULTURE.

CHAPTER 12

PRINCIPLE TWELVE: MIRACLES, SIGNS, AND WONDERS

There are many people walking, talking, and breathing who have experienced a miracle unknowingly. They call it happenstance or coincidence. It never dawns on them that there is something that is working behind the scenes every single day of our lives. Different religions call that intelligence many different things. I am going to stick to what I know to be true of the power of the Holy Spirit. I will never be able to separate miracles from Jesus Christ. He worked them daily. He flowed in a level of ascension that left an example for those that are Disciples of Christ. He was beyond religion and tore down the systems that brought forth more bondage than freedom. Though we have Christianity, it was not started by Him. It includes his teachings, but it is classified as a religion, something he didn't incorporate in His messages. We have moved far away from what He actually desired and now it is time to return home.

Growing up in a small town, and attending a local Baptist church gave me a foundation of word, doctrine, order, and organization. At some point I had to move away from that Baptist box and move into more knowledge. While I cherish everything I learned and to this day give great honor to my Pastor Reverend James E. Lee Jr., I knew there was more I needed. I needed more because I was going to do more. I didn't know as a 10-year-old getting baptized on August 11, 1985 that I would become who I am today. I was reared to grow into my destiny. I wanted to see miracles that I heard others talk about. I wanted to see the supernatural in healings that were transformative. I knew that if I kept that desire, I would see them. I did see them. As I matriculated through my ministry journey, I saw people healed of cancer, I saw blind eyes open, I saw deaf ears unstopped, and I saw people suffering with mental illness healed. I saw these miracles with the belief that the supernatural was not an everyday occurrence, but just a sporadic occurrence. I was never taught that they could happen every day. In my curiosity for truth I searched the Scripture and what I found was eye-opening. One Scripture opened my eyes to DAILY MIRACLES, SIGNS, AND WONDERS.

Acts 2:22 (KJV)

"Ye men of Israel, hear these words;
Jesus of Nazareth, a man approved of
God among you by miracles and wonders and
signs, which God did by him in the midst of
you, as ye yourselves also know:"

Acts of the Apostles is filled with accounts of miracles. This particular scripture grabbed my attention because it connected a person with the supernatural power to perform miracles, signs, and wonders. These things were not experienced sporadically. All throughout this book are account after account of miracles, healings, supernatural signs, and wonders.

The Old Testament is also filled with miraculous accounts. A barren Sarah, Abraham's wife had a grievous obstacle to overcome. She had a promise of a son but was 90-years-old and barren. But the promise was made manifest…

Genesis 21:7 (KJV)

"And she said, Who would have said unto Abraham, that Sarah should have given children suck? for I have born *him* a son in his old age."

Miracles were for those THAT BELIEVED! It was experienced by those that had a trust in the mighty works of Yahweh. Even if they wavered in doubt, he understood how to produce something that removed their unbelief. I knew at that very pivotal moment that not only could I witness miracles, but I would be a catalyst for manifestation with my belief in the supernatural. I would not only witness but I would participate in the manifestation of miracles. This process began with the importance of establishing a consistent prayer life. I knew I needed an intimate relationship with the Holy Spirit to flow in limitless power.

I spent many years of my early ministry known to be a prayer intercessor. People would call me and I would see powerful signs of my belief joined with another to produce manifestation. I not only believed the Scripture, I put action to it. I specifically recall one of the times I needed a miracle. My oldest son was born and as the doctor looked at his bloodwork, he said it appeared he had Sickle Cell anemia. Well, my heart dropped simultaneously as the Holy Spirit stood up. I told the doctor to give me two weeks and we'd run the test again. I took my son home, who had no symptoms and I began to pray and anoint him daily. When we went back to the doctor, he was shocked. The original bloodwork was totally different from the current bloodwork. What was present before was no longer there. Miracles can happen DAILY!

As we ascend spiritually, we will experience divine favor, supernatural doors open, divine opportunities emerge, and blessings are multiplied. Will life be like roses? Absolutely not. Will everything always turn out on miraculous proportions? You already know that answer. One thing is for sure, you have access to this power by going within.

I am not sure what you call the Holy Spirit within; you have that choice and I am not here to debate terminologies or religion. What I am sure of is that we have this in common, we all desire to flow in the supernatural power that not only defies logic, but brings peace. Having connection with the supernatural returns us to our original form. We are a spirit in a body. We are eternal beings, we participate in our ascension by embracing our ability to BE AND DO. We do what ascended masters like Jesus Christ did. You get to choose how high you will go or how much you will use this supernatural power to design your life. LIFE IS INDEED WHAT YOU MAKE IT!

PROPHETIC DECREEE: YOU WILL MANIFEST MIRACLES, SIGNS, AND WONDERS PERPETUALLY!

www.ingramcontent.com/pod-product-compliance
Lightning Source LLC
Chambersburg PA
CBHW071333190426
43193CB00041B/1771